Memory Improvement Mastery

Dale Owen

Copyright 2018 by Dale Owen - All rights reserved.

The following Book is reproduced below with the goal of providing information that is as accurate and reliable as possible. Regardless, purchasing this Book can be seen as consent to the fact that both the publisher and the author of this book are in no way experts on the topics discussed within and that any recommendations or suggestions that are made herein are for entertainment purposes only. Professionals should be consulted as needed prior to undertaking any of the action endorsed herein.

This declaration is deemed fair and valid by both the American Bar Association and the Committee of Publishers Association and is legally binding throughout the United States.

Furthermore, the transmission, duplication or reproduction of any of the following work including specific information will be considered an illegal act irrespective of if it is done electronically or in print. This extends to creating a secondary or tertiary copy of the work or a recorded copy and is only allowed with express written consent from the Publisher. All additional right reserved.

The information in the following pages is broadly considered to be a truthful and accurate account of facts and as such any inattention, use or misuse of the information in question by the reader will render any resulting actions solely under their purview. There are no scenarios in which the publisher or the original author of this work can be in any fashion deemed liable for any hardship or damages that may befall them after undertaking information described herein.

Additionally, the information in the following pages is intended only for informational purposes and should thus be thought of as universal. As befitting its nature, it is presented without assurance regarding its prolonged validity or interim quality. Trademarks that are mentioned are done without written consent and can in no way be considered an endorsement from the trademark holder.

Contents

Introduction 1

Understanding How The Mind Works 4

    The Brain and How It Works to Memorize Things 5

    The Flaws of the Brain and the Mind 10

    Memory Consolidation 13

    Why and How We Forget and Remember Certain Things 17

    Attention 18

    Consolidating the Memory 19

    Memory Recall 20

    Priming 21

    Mood Memory 22

    Blanking Out 22

    Duration Neglect 24

    Why Some People Remember More Than Others 25

What About Photographic Memories.................. 28

How Age Can Affect the Memory...................... 32

What Causes Memory Problems 38

Possible Causes of Memory Problems.................. 38

Identifying Memory Problems at Home, Work, and in Relationships 42

Are You Burnt Out Mentally? What Are the Signs? 46

Remembering Names and Faces.......................... 52

How Focus, Concentration, and Observation Affect the Memory Process 56

Memory Recall.. 58

Let's Test Your Memory 66

Memory Improvement Techniques And Exercises 70

Stop Multitasking 70

Focusing Your Attention 73

Avoiding Cramming... 74

Be Organized and Structured.............................. 75

Relate the Information Back to Things You Know 76

Read the Information Out Loud 77

Trying Meditation..78

Live a Life That Is Blessed and Happy 82

Getting Enough Sleep...85

Playing Brain Games...87

Master a New Skill 90

Trying Mnemonic Devices..................................92

The Method of Loci 93

Acronyms...94

Rhymes..96

Organization and Chunking................................97

Imagery..99

The 4 Details Exercise......................................100

Number Brain Exercises...................................102

Doing Recall in Your Mind...............................103

The Metronome Clapping Exercise 104

Create Your Own Memory Palace 105

- Learn a New Language 107
- Working with a Mind Map 108
- Playing a Sport 109

Memory Improving in Your Day to Day Life ... 112
- Exercising 113
- Socializing 114
- Keep Doing Mental Activities 115
- Organizing Your Life 116
- Eating Well 118
- Sleeping Well 120
- Medications That Can Help with Memory Improvement 124

Rebooting and Refreshing Your Brain 128
- Mindfulness 129
- Visual Tasks 130
- Chewing Gum 131
- Belly Breathing 133

Conclusion 135

Introduction

In the following chapters we will discuss everything that you need to know in order to improve your memories ability to remember things such as dates, people, events, and other important things that go on in our daily lives. All of us struggle with our memory on occasion. We often forget where our keys are, or where we have left our wallet when it's time to leave the house. We sometimes even overschedule ourselves due to forgetting things like a particular event that is due to happen in our lives. Failing to remember things often can usually lead to upsetting people, causing ourselves to feel let down as a result.

Having a lapse in memory on occasion is normal. Sometimes we aren't able to encode the information in the way that we should, or we just aren't focusing on the information enough because we are so busy and occupied by other things. However, when these things start to happen on a more regular basis, then this can cause some problems. When these problems arise, it is natural and perfectly normal to start looking for some easy ways that we can improve our memory and make the issues go away.

This guide is going to spend some time talking about how the memory works and the different ways that you can improve your memory. First, we start out with an understanding of how the mind works. We will talk about why we forget certain things, why some people are better at remembering than others, and even how age is going to affect the way that memory works. From there, we will do a discussion on what will cause most memory problems and what we are able to do to improve these problems so that they don't start to cause more issues or get worse further down the line.

Then, we are going to move onto some of the various techniques that you can use to help improve your memory and ensure that it works the way that you want. This chapter is full of various ideas that you can use that help you to really work on improving how well the memory is able to work. We will then finish off with information on simple things that you can implement into your daily life to improve your memory as well as some basics to help reboot and recharge the mind any time that you need.

All of us want to work to improve our memory and ensure that it works in the best way possible. There are a variety of tools and techniques that we can use to make this happen.

There are plenty of books you could of chosen on this subject on the market—but thanks again for choosing this one! Every effort has been made to ensure that it is full of as much useful information as possible.

Chapter 1

Understanding How The Mind Works

The mind has long been thought of as a mysterious thing. There is a lot that we still don't know when it comes to the brain. We don't fully understand how it stores memories—even though we are finding out that a lot of facts out there are wrong and that there isn't just one place in the brain that holds onto these memories.

Being able to understand how the mind works and how we form and store memories can be critical when it comes to ensuring that we get the most out of improving our memory. This chapter is going to take some time to discuss the different ways the mind works, how we are able to memorize things, how memories are formed, why some people can remember better than others, how aging can affect the way that we remember things, and even a discussion on photographic memory to help us get started.

The Brain and How It Works to Memorize Things

The more that you are able to learn about the memory, the better that you are going to be able to understand the best way to improve your own memory. Most of us are going to talk about memory like it is something that we have—like lots of hair or bad eyes. However, the memory isn't going to exist in the same way that a part of our body exists simply because it's not something that we are able to touch. Instead, memory is a concept that refers to the process of remembering.

There has been a lot of research done to discuss the memory and how it works. In the past, there were many experts who found it easiest to describe the memory like a filing cabinet that had different folders for each memory, and that is how all the memories were stored. Other experts would say its like a supercomputer in the brain that would hold these memories.

However, today, many researchers believe that the memory for humans can be even more elusive and complex than was thought possible in the past. In fact, our memories aren't even stored in one particular part of the brain over another. The memories are going to be stored all across the brain, which can make this system even more complex to deal with.

To start this section out, let's think back to what you had for breakfast this morning. If you had an image of eggs and bacon, or maybe some cereal shows up, this doesn't mean that you dredged it up from some neural alleyway. What really happened was that this memory showed up because it was a result of an incredibly complex constructive power, something that all of us are able to do, that reassembled the memory impressions from a web-like pattern of cells that aren't found in just one area of the brain but throughout all the different parts.

In fact, what we know of the memory right now is it's just a group of systems that come together in order to create, store, and recall our memories. When the brain is able to process this information normally, all of these systems are going to work together in order to provide us with some cohesive thoughts. Because of this, what may seem like a single memory to us is very complex.

Let's say that you are thinking about some kind of object. For this, we are going to think about a pen. Your brain is then going to retrieve the name of the object, the shape it is, the function, and even the sounds that the pen can make when it writes on the page. Each part of the memory of the pen is going to show up from different regions of the brain, this also comes from different areas to form the whole picture. It is only recently that neurologists are starting to understand the different ways that these memories are being reassembled when we call them up.

When you are looking to remember something, you will need to go to the unconscious level of the brain and retrieve the information so it comes back to the conscious mind. While most people believe that they have either a good or bad memory, most people have strengths and weaknesses when it comes to what they can and can't remember. If you do have some troubles with remembering a certain topic, unless you have other diseases or factors at play, this usually is not indicative of the whole system of the memory not working.

Let's look at an example here. We want to try to remember where we put our eyeglasses. When you head to bed at night, you need to register where your put your glasses. You need to focus and pay attention to whereabouts you have set them on the bedside table before bed. You then need to also have awareness of where you are putting them, or it is impossible to remember this location the next morning. Next, all of this information is retained, and ready for you to retrieve it, later on. If your memory and the system with it is working properly, then when it is time to wake up the next morning, you will know the exact spot where you left the glasses.

Now, if you woke up the next morning and you forgot where your glasses are, then there are a few different things that may have happened, including:

1. You may not have really registered where you placed those glasses in the first place.
2. You may have had trouble retaining the information that you just registered.
3. You may be struggling to retrieve the memory in an accurate manner.

What this means is that if you want to stop forgetting the location of your eyeglasses, then you need to make sure that each of these stages of the remembering process is working as it should be. If you have forgotten something, it is likely that you weren't able to encode it effectively. Often this happens because you became distracted while the encoding process took place. When you forget where you place the glasses, this can be a sign that the location of the glasses didn't end up in the memory to start with.

Distractions that show up when you try to remember something new can sometimes get in the way of helping the brain encode the memories. If something isn't encoded, then you won't be able to encode it later on. If you have ever taken the time to remember something once, and you weren't able to, but then you could remember that item later on, this is a sign that there was a mismatch between your retrieval cues and the encoding of the information you wanted to remember.

The Flaws of the Brain and the Mind

Our brains and minds can be marvelous things. They help us in our daily functioning, completing unfinished work, getting us to and from places, making decisions, and so much more. Our minds help us to store memories and learn something new almost every day. But there are some limitations that come into play as well.

There are so many stimuli that come at us from every direction all day long. From sounds, sights, smells to things we touch and everything in between. If our brains even tried to take in all of this, we would be overwhelmed and wouldn't be able to get anything done at all. Because of this, our minds have to adjust and learn what is important and what isn't as important, turning off everything else to ensure that we are able to just take in what is the most important.

Now, often the brain is going to take over and do this automatically for us. As we go along our day, we find that we are able to just get things done without thinking about it at all. For example, when we head into work, how much do you really notice along the way? Do you recognize all the cars that pass you, what music is on the radio, or anything else other than the route you are taking? There is a ton of stuff that you pass on a drive to work, this is often the same when it comes to other tasks that you do. But unless something out of the normal happens, like an accident that delays and makes you late to work, it is likely you will just go to work and not think anything more about it.

You can learn how to focus on the things that you want to remember. Going back to the example of the ride to work, the next time you head out, move your focus onto the drive, taking in everything and seeing it as important. This will open your mind and your eyes to things that you never saw in the past, and allow you to train the mind into memorizing things that you usually wouldn't have.

The brain can sometimes be distorted by our emotions, both when you are experiencing the event and later on when the memory comes back out in the recall. With the first instance, you may find that your brain will distort some things based on the mood. For example, if you were feeling elated because of something, you may have a memory of a great day at work or a fantastic drive through traffic, even if these weren't that great of things.

When your memories get distorted based on your current mood, this often leads you to think about situations and things based on that particular mood. For example, if your current mood is that your sad and depressed, then you may run into the issue of only being able to remember the bad stuff and sadness that our memory lets us think about.

Our brain is a powerful tool. We are able to control it, but since there is just so much going on in our lives and around us, it is sometimes hard to get it to make and store memories in the correct manner. Learning how to control the mind and to get the most out of it can really make a big difference when it comes to how well we are able to store our own memories and remember things later on.

Memory Consolidation

Memory consolidation is going to be a process that is needed in coding memory so that you can retrieve it later on. Without this consolidation process, there isn't any way for you to store information in your brain, which is something that needs to happen if you want to form and store memories to use later on. Consolidation is something that you can observe in many species of animals, and each one seems to have a different capacity for forming and storing these new memories. There are several things that are able to interfere with the consolidation of memories.

The process of memory consolidation is going to begin within a few minutes on the synaptic level whenever the brain encounters something new, whether it is new or not, and then takes the time to interact with it. System consolidation is going to happen in the long term, usually over weeks and months when the brain works to develop new pathways so it is easier to access that memory. The stronger these pathways are, the easier it is for you to recall them later on.

Research that has been done on the brain shows how memories aren't just stored in one particular part of the brain, but they are spread out in various locations. Consolidation is the process of making these spread out memories more accessible, basically creating a good index or map to the brain to ensure that you are able to retrieve any of the memories that are needed when you need them most.

Once your brain has gone through and stored a memory, it can recall that memory at any time you want. Initially, it was believed that memories were stored there permanently. But in recent years, researchers have learned that these memories need to be reconsolidated every time that you call them out. Memories can become labile. What this means is that the memories are fragile and it is possible for you to disrupt them any time you recall them. The process of reconsolidation returns these recalled memories back to the right place in the brain so that you are able to use them again.

There are a few different functions that can come into play when we talk about memory consolidation. First off, the hippocampus is often going to play a very important role when it comes to forming memories and then storing them. Other parts of the brain will help out as well, based on the type of memory that is involved in the process.

For example, REM sleep, or rapid eye movement, can come into play when it is time for the consolidation of memories. This may show that this process happens when we spend time sleeping and refreshing the brain. Without proper amounts of sleep, it may be difficult for you to consolidate the memories in the proper manner. If you are suffering with the issue of remembering things and holding memories for the long-term, it may be time for you to consider changing your sleeping patterns so you can see better results with your memory.

Another thing to look at is some of the phenomena that researchers have been able to observe when you learn. While this process of consolidation is normally going to take a longer period of time, there are studies of people who were involved in learning tasks have shown that the brain does have the power to consolidate a memory successfully in an hour or less in certain cases.

The methods that are used in order to present the information can make a big difference in how long that process takes—and the number of times you repeat the information can help as well. Repeating the same information to yourself over and over can cause some synaptic changes that will then lead to rapid consolidation of memory. This could help show why recitation can help you to learn and keep things in your memory for a long period of time.

Why and How We Forget and Remember Certain Things

One of the normal functions of emotion is to help enhance certain memories so that we are able to recall these experiences, especially when they have more relevance or importance for our survival. These emotions are going to be similar to what we do with a highlighter pen. They will go through and emphasize certain aspects of experiences to make these more memorable for us. Memory formation is going to involve the registering of information, processing and storing that information, and then retrieving it later on.

Emotion is going to help affect all of the phases of memory formation. We are able to remember things better when there is some kind of strong emotion tied to it. This is why we are better able to remember our wedding day or the birth of a child or our graduation but have a hard time remembering where we put the keys. The keys have no emotions tied to them, but the other events do. Let's take a look at the way that emotion can affect the formation of memory:

Attention

First, we need to look at the attention that we give an event. Attention is going to help guide our focus to select what is the most relevant to our lives, and often it is going to be associated with novelty. Nothing is going to move our focus over to a certain event like a surprise, for example.

Think of it this way. While we may find that we enjoy a particular conversation one time, if we went back through and had the exact same conversation a second time, we would find it to be bull. The emotional intensity is going to act as a way to narrow the scope of our attention so that a few objects can be emphasized, while the rest are ignored or not focused on. Since we are not able to focus on everything that happens in our whole lives, being able to focus on a very narrow area allows for optimal use of the limited attention that we have.

Consolidating the Memory

Most of the information that we are able to acquire is going to be forgotten and it never makes it on the long journey to becoming a long-term memory. There is just too much for us to try and remember on a day to day basis, that it doesn't make sense to try and fit it all into the long-term memory. When we start to learn a problem that is complex, our short-term memory will open up, like an automatic action that happens for us. But then, how does the brain decide which of the memories in the short-term memory get erased and which ones get to move into more permanent storage?

Events and memories that have some kind of emotion behind them, especially really strong emotions, are the ones that are going to be more likely to get stored in the long-term memory. The stress hormones of cortisol and epinephrine are there to enhance your memory, which ables it to consolidate the contents of that memory. When we look at this in an evolutionary way, it makes logical sense for us to imprint dangerous situations with some extra clarity because this allows us to avoid some of the harmful stuff or the things that causes us stress and other issues, and then avoid those situations later.

Memory Recall

Memories of experiences that are painful and emotional are going to linger much longer than those that would cause us actual physical pain. Contrary to what we learned in the past about sticks and stones may break our bones, but words never hurt us, evidence shows that feelings being hurt can be much worse than any physical pain. We never seem to forget how we made them feel.

What is really interesting here when it comes to our emotions and memories is that some common pain killers, such as acetaminophen found in Tylenol, may not only be effective when it comes to physical pain that we feel, like sore muscles and headaches, it can also be effective with emotional pain.

Priming

Past memories are often going to be triggered, also known as primed, by the environment that you are in. Priming refers to activating behavior through the power of unconscious suggestion. There has been previous research that shows how people who were made to think of self—discipline (they had to work on unscrambling sentences about this topic), were immediately able to make more future oriented snack choices compared to those who were given the same exercise, but on self-indulgence.

In the case above, the goal stored in the long-term memory was retrieved and then put into our working or short-term memory. The way that we bring these out and influence the results that we get over time. This is similar to the idea of going into the library and automatically talking in a quiet voice, because that we was taught from an early age what we should do when visiting libraries.

Mood Memory

The emotional state that we are in at that current moment can really facilitate the recall of experiences that may have had a similar emotional tone for us. So, if we are in a good or happy mood, we are more likely to recall happy and pleasant events. If we are in an angry or sad mood, then these are the kinds of memories we are going to recall.

For example, you may be more likely to recall some positive experiences in your childhood if you are currently in a good mood. But when you are in a bad mood, you are more primed to think about negative thoughts and emotions. Changing yourself from one mood to the other and changing up the memories that you have at that time can sometimes be a challenge for people.

Blanking Out

You may find that high levels of stress can lead to issues with a memory deficit. This is why it is a common experience to blank out mentally when you have a very high pressure situation, like a test or an interview, going on at that time. Many times we struggle with remembering anything when we are stressed out and dealing with a lot of different things on our plate.

For the most part, anxiety can influence the way that our brains function in what is known as an inverted U-curve, or a curvilinear manner. This is a phenomenon that is known as the Yerkes-Dodson law. What this basically means is that when levels of arousal are too low, such as when we are bored, and when these levels of arousal tend to be too high, such as when we are dealing with fear or anxiety, our performance is more likely to suffer as a result.

When we are in situations of boredom or otherwise not being aroused mentally, the mind becomes very unfocused and doesn't know how to proceed. But when we are in situations that are overly stimulated and too hard to handle, the focus of our attention is going to be too narrow, and this can cause us to lose out on a lot of the information. Having a moderate amount of arousal is necessary to ensure that we aren't bored and unfocused, but that we can still catch the details that we need that are around us.

Duration Neglect

Another thing to consider is the duration neglect. The method that we use to remember events isn't always going to be made up of a total of every individual moment. Instead, most people find that they are going to remember and overemphasize the peak moment, the worst moment, the best moments, and the last moment. In the process, they are going to neglect the duration of the experience as a whole.

This is why we may have a great time at a party, but then one small thing at the end can ruin the whole experience. Think back to your last vacation. If it lasted for a week or more, there is going to be a lot of information to keep track of and too much for you to reasonably evaluate to tell if it is enjoyable. So, you would use the duration neglect, also known as the peak end rule, to help you heavily way the best moments of the trip with the most recent moment of that trip, to help you come up with an evaluation.

So basically, what this means is that we are going to rely heavily on our own emotions to tell us whether we will need to remember something or not. The more that a memory is tied to a specific emotion, especially a strong one like happiness, sadness, and anger, the more likely we are to remember it.

Why Some People Remember More Than Others

Every person is going to have a different kind of memory. This is going to depend on a number of factors, including your genetics, your age, and how much you stimulate and work on the mind. If you can work and keep yourself healthy and doing well, and you work to regularly challenge your brain, then you will find that it is easier to remember things compared to others.

First, we need to look at age. For some people, aging can cause their memories to go down a little. If you make sure to challenge yourself on a regular basis, get outside and move around, do some mental challenges on occasion, and eat a healthy diet, then the memory loss is not going to be that big of a deal. In fact, healthy adults can easily keep their memory as sharp as it was when they were younger, no matter how old they are.

For some people, it is all about genetics. If you have a family history of dementia and Alzheimer's, then you may find that your more prone to memory decline more than other people. This doesn't mean that all is lost and you are never going to be able to keep your brain and your mind sharp. It just means that you may need more mental practice and more challenges to keep the brain working well. Even then, you may not be able to get the memory up to what other people can do. But you do still have some control, so don't just sit back and let the deterioration occur over time just because you think it is inevitable that your memory will be gone.

Finally, you can always work on stimulating the brain and making it work harder. The biggest reason that the memory starts to fade is that the brain is not getting the workout that it needs. We assume that the brain will just stay strong and smart without any work on our part. But if we never work the brain by doing something new, or we never focus on going somewhere new, learning something new, or providing a challenge for the brain, then we are just going to end up with memory issues.

There are a lot of different ways that you can make sure your brain gets stronger and that, despite age and other factors, you won't end up losing your memory. You can work on mind puzzles and games. You can go out and explore some new places and meet new people, even traveling to help open up the mind. You can learn a new language or something else that has always interested you to help your mind stay sharp.

Some of the people who have better memories have this because they actively work on it. They may employ various memory and thinking techniques on a regular basis. They may spend more time reading and enjoying the arts, and may get out and explore new places and see new things. They also keep their environment stimulating, rather than just sitting around watching television all day. Some of the other factors can come into play on occasion, but we do have a bit of control when it comes to how well our brains and memories can function. If we are proactive, we are more likely to see that our memories actually improve and we will see some amazing results that others are jealous of as well.

What About Photographic Memories

One thing that we need to take some time to consider here is the idea of photographic memory. This kind of memory is quite a bit different from what we are used to when we talk about the memory. While most of us struggle to remember lists or other information for a very long time, people with a photographic memory can often remember things years down the line, and they will remember it perfectly no matter how long has passed.

A person who has a photographic memory is someone who is able to remember events and scenes as detailed and precise images. There have been a lot of studies that suggest that having a truly photographic memory is pretty much non-existence. But there are people who have what is known as an eidetic memory. This is similar, but a little bit different. These two terms are very similar though and most of the people you meet who have really strong memories will fit into the category of eidetic memory.

For those who believe that there is a photographic memory and that some people do have such a thing, it is thought that these people are able to store information, usually in the form of a detailed image, and then that person can pull it out and recall what happened at will. For example, this kind of memory would allow someone to describe a painting in detail after just seeing it one time, or they may be able to recite out whole passages from a book that they had just glanced at.

Now, some people are believed to be able to work hard and gain the skills. There are different techniques that can be utilized in order to make this a technique that works well for you. But this means that you have to develop the skill, not that it is one you are born with.

On the other hand, there are those who have an eidetic memory. These individuals are going to store visual information with a very high level of precision. This allows them to repeat information with a ton of details, but they can usually only do this for a short period of time after they see the material. So, if they just saw a painting briefly, they may be able to describe it with a lot of detail. But they wouldn't be able to do the same thing down the line.

Eidetic memory can be found in almost anyone, but it is the most common in children, and it often fades with age. The reason for this, or at least the reason that most researchers think that this happens, is because most children are going to store the information they encounter in a visual way, unlike adults who focus more on the verbal.

For those individuals who have more of an eidetic memory, whether it is from children or adults, they appear to store the information in ways that are very different fundamentally, from the way that we will store memories. This allows them to have a better chance of recalling the information later on. This type of memory is not going to be the same as a photographic memory, a word that we hear a lot but doesn't really happen, but they may appear as similar to the outsider.

There has been a lot of people throughout history who have been able to demonstrate an astounding ability to memorize things, whether it was the lines of many plays, to the details of visual scenes. These individuals may seem like they had a photographic memory, but in reality, it is more likely that they spent years training themselves to remember things like this.

For those who work in various fields were memory is a key to their success, such as with musicians, painters, and actors, there are many different memory tricks can help make things easier. These individuals may do a better job of remembering things and utilizing those tricks, but often it is more through hard work and some dedication, and not memory magic like we may think.

This is good news for most people though. It means that we can also learn to make our memories sharper and to ensure that we are going to be able to bring back information at any time that it is needed. You don't have to feel bad because you don't have a photographic memory. You don't have to let things slide just because you are getting older. You can still utilize these same techniques and tricks to help make strengthen your brain power.

How Age Can Affect the Memory

There have been many studies done to look at the effects of aging on our memories. Many people claim that they have a hard time remembering things when they age and feel like there isn't much that they can do to stop this progression and help them out. While some people do experience issues with dementia, Alzheimer's and other types of memory loss as they age, the normal healthy person may not have to worry about aging as much when it comes to your memory and how strong it is.

Yes, many times you may notice that you forget the keys or why you walked into a room, and remembering names starts to become more and more difficult. But this doesn't mean that our memories have to fade and that it is only a matter of time before we can remember anything. No matter what our age is, we are able to still remember things and keep our memory sharp.

Researchers have a few different theories when it comes to what's behind the mind deterioration that can happen when you start to age, but most suspect that as we age, this causes major cell loss in a tiny region found in the front of the brain that can lead to a drop in the production of a neurotransmitter known as acetylcholine. This transmitter is very important when it comes to your memory and to learning overall.

In addition, a few of the parts of the brain that you need and are essential to your memory can be very vulnerable when it comes to aging. One area, which is the hippocampus, is going to start losing about 5 percent of all its nerve cells with each decade that passes. This means that you could potentially lose about 20 percent of these nerve cells by the time you get to your 80s unless you are careful and work to preserve them. In addition, it is thought that the brain itself, without the proper exercises, can start shrinking and becoming less efficient as you age as well.

These are natural things that can occur to your brain as you age. There are also other things that you could do that may speed up the decline. For example, if you have a genetic predisposition to memory problems or other brain diseases, then this can make things worse. If you were ever exposed to poisons this can cause problems. Also things like drinking and smoking can play a big part in causing your memory to lose function. Each of these things, plus more, can all speed up the decline of your memory.

As you age, there are also some physical changes that make the brain not work as efficiently as before and this makes it hard for you to remember in an efficient manner. However, this doesn't mean that losing your memory and ending up with dementia is something that you just have to prepare for and have no say in the matter. In fact, while there are some abilities that do tend to decline with age, overall memory can still remain strong for most people, even when they progress though their 70s.

Research has already shown us that the average 70-year-old is going to be able to perform just as well on certain cognitive tests as their 20-year-old counterparts. It has been found that those in their 60s and 70s are able to do much better with the verbal intelligence than younger people. Studies have also shown that many of the memory problems that some older people deal with can be lessened, and in some cases reversed.

In one of these studies, nursing home populations were studied. This found that patients were actually able to make large improvements with their memory when they were given rewards and challenges along the way. Mental stimulation and physical exercise can also work to help improve the mental function of everyone, no matter what age they are.

In another study that was done on animals, it was suggested that you can stimulate the brain in order to stop the nerve cells from shrinking, and this could even help to increase the size of the brain in some cases. Studies showed that rats that lived in enriched environments, or ones that have lots of challenges and toys, are going to have a larger outer brain along with healthier and bigger brain cells. And those that were given a lot of mental exercises tended to have more dendrites, which are the part of the brain that makes it easier for the cells to communicate back and forth with each other.

How does this correlate back to humans? Research has also been done on memory for humans as they age. It has found that in later years, having an environment that is stimulating and maybe brings in a few challenges on occasion, can help to grow those dendrites so the brain is able to communicate between the different cells. But if the environment around the person, no matter their age, becomes dull and boring, then this can impede the growth of these dendrites.

The important thing to remember here is that as you age, you may not be able to learn or remember things quite as quickly as you did in the past, such as when you were in school, but you will be able to learn and remember things just as well, if not better, than you did before. Often the issues that come with aging and your memory have nothing to do with simply aging, it is more likely caused because the brain is not used on a regular basis. No matter what age you are, make sure that you stimulate your brain and keep it active. If you can do this, rather then memory loss is not going to be an issue that you have to deal with.

Chapter 2

WHAT CAUSES MEMORY PROBLEMS

Memory problems are something that everyone deals with on occasion. People will often end up worrying about misplacing things, or not being able to remember a certain important date that they should. This is pretty common and is going to happen to everyone at some point or another.

In this chapter, we are going to take a look at some of the main memory problems that you may face, some of the possible causes of these memory problems, and more.

Possible Causes of Memory Problems

A bit of memory loss is common in most of us. Maybe we were distracted when we met someone new, and then we couldn't remember their name later on. New mothers often forget things as they try to adjust to the new sleeping schedule with a baby. Maybe we are tired or stressed out from work causing it to become hard to handle the memories and remember the things that we should. There are a lot of different causes for memory loss. But the good news is that most of us are able to fix some of these issues with a few minor adjustments. Let's take a look at some of the most common reasons that you may be dealing with memory loss.

First, medication can sometimes cause a bit of memory loss. There are several over the counter and prescription medications that will interfere with our memory, and even cause memory loss. Some of the most common culprits of this include pain medications for surgery, sleeping pills, muscle relaxants, anti-anxiety medications, antihistamines, and antidepressants.

Drugs, tobacco and alcohol usage, can all cause some issues with your memory if you use them in excess. Excessive alcohol consumption on a regular basis has long been seen as a major cause of memory loss. In addition, smoking can harm your mind and memory because it will reduce the amount of oxygen that the brain gets. Studies have shown that those who smoke will often have more trouble putting a name to the face compared to those who don't smoke. In addition, illicit drugs can be dangerous to your memory because they will change up the way the chemicals react in the brain, making it much harder to recall memories.

If you are low on sleep, then your memories may be affected. The quality and the quantity of sleep are very important when it comes to memory. Not getting enough sleep on a regular basis, or if you wake up often during the night, this can lead to fatigue, which will really interfere with your brain's ability to consolidate and retrieve information when it's needed later on.

Stress and depression are some more causes to memory loss. When you have feelings of depression, it is hard for you to focus and pay attention to anything, which is going to affect the memory. In addition, anxiety and stress can also get in the way of how much you are able to concentrate. When you are tense, or your mind feels distracted and overstimulated, the ability to remember things will suffer. Also stress that is caused by some kind of emotional trauma can lead to memory loss as well.

There are some studies that suggest having a nutritional deficiency in certain nutrients can cause you to have some issues with your memory. For example, if your diet is low in high quality fats and proteins, it can be a cause to impairing your memory. In addition, being low on vitamin B12 and B1 can specifically cause some issues with your memory.

If you have been in an accident or another situation where you have suffered a head injury, then this could be a cause of memory impairment and damage that could affect you greatly. Any kind of severe hit to your head, such as from an accident, has been shown a lot of the time to cause some sort of injury leading to long term and short term memory loss. Depending on the situation and the severity of the injury, the memory may be able to improve over time.

It is also possible to suffer from memory loss from dementia, and this can lead to diseases like Alzheimer's. These are much more serious issues to deal with, and most of the time, the memory loss that you are dealing with is not going to be that bad. If you are dealing with dementia or any of the diseases associated with it, it is important to talk with your doctor right away to see what you are able to do. Since most memory issues are not going to be this bad, which allows you to improve them over time.

Identifying Memory Problems at Home, Work, and in Relationships

All of us will be forgetful at times. Just when we think we can remember the name of someone, it often will escape us. We try to remember things like where we put that important paperwork or our car keys, and yet we still can't find them. Forgetting things on occasion is not really a sign of a memory problem. Often it is just a sign that we weren't focusing enough on the issue at hand, and so the mind wasn't able to properly encode it at that time.

However, there are times when you may be dealing with memory problems, and it is important to learn the best ways to deal with these issues. Without working on the right techniques and with the right tools from the beginning, it is possible that the memory issues will become worse.

Now, there are some early memory issues that you may deal with. These are usually not too severe, and if you just experience one or two on occasion, there isn't much to be concerned about. But when the issues start to happen more frequently, or you experience quite a few of them, it is time to make changes to ensure your memory loss gets better, rather than worse. Some of the early signs that you should watch out for when it comes to memory problems include:

- ❖ Your personality may change. Maybe you start to get angry for no reason and your behavior all of a sudden becomes inappropriate.
- ❖ You commonly misplace items and can't ever seem to find them.
- ❖ You start to have trouble with the words you use. It's more than a slip of the tongue and can make communication difficult with others.

- ❖ You start to get lost or confused if you go off course, and sometimes even on routes that you are familiar with.
- ❖ It often becomes more difficult for you to make decisions.
- ❖ You run into more difficulty with any task that requires you to put in some thought. This could include something as simple as balancing your check book.
- ❖ Difficulty doing well at work. This can be due to the fact that you have more issues getting along with people, or because you can't remember the details of a particular project and often start to make more mistakes.
- ❖ Forgetting important dates or double booking yourself on certain dates because you've forgotten about prior engagements.

These memory problems can easily start to creep into your life and can make things more difficult. When it comes to your home life, things can become difficult because you are always loosing things, forgetting how to complete certain tasks, and even getting lost on routes that are familiar to you. This will usually give you the feeling of being trapped in your own home, and maybe can cause you to become anxious because you are constantly wondering what you are forgetting about.

Memory problems can cause issues with your work life as well. Since you are worried about forgetting things, and worried that people will start noticing that you forget things, you may feel tenser and have trouble getting along with others. You may start to forget important details about a project or something else that you are working on, causing friction as others will have to pick up the work.

It is even possible to run into some issues with your personal life or your relationships. Often relationships will be affected by things like not being able to remember certain dates or important events that are going on in your partners life, and also other that involve money and paying bills.

Memory problems can affect almost every part of your life. It may seem like such a simple thing, and you may not feel that forgetting a thing here or there is a big deal, but as things progress, it can start to affect every part of your life. The good news is that you can work on these things. Just because you are already forgetting a few things here and there doesn't mean that you are doomed to just see more and more memory loss. If you work on strengthening your mind and working on your memory, you will be able to improve the different aspects of your life as well.

Are You Burnt Out Mentally? What Are the Signs?

Mental burnout is sometimes a common occurrence when your brain is overactive. Feelings of being overwhelmed by all of the responsibilities and tasks that you have to handle on a daily basis can make you feel lots of frustration and mental unrest. You will often have emotions of envy of others who seem to be more laid back and relaxed than you are, and your levels of mental stress can make things worse.

When you spend a ton of mental effort on any task, this will usually lead you to become mentally exhausted. While this does happen occasionally even for those who are otherwise healthy, it can be manageable in the beginning, but over time, it can cause a lot of issues, especially when it comes to maintaining your focus. This can leave you with low concentration levels and leads to more mistakes in your work than normal. You can even start to feel things like depression, irritation, and stress which just leads you to a downward spiral, and can affect your overall health in no time.

Mental exhaustion is often recognized when the individual feels burnt out from excess and long-term stress. While this is something that we all experience at least a little bit on occasion, the symptoms can become worse over time if you don't pay attention and work on it. If mental exhaustion carries on for too long, it can manifest itself into other symptoms such as behavioral, emotional, and physical. Some of the different side effects that you could experience when dealing with mental burnout include:

- ❖ Physical symptoms: There are a number of physical symptoms that you may experience if the burnout is going on for too long. You may feel like you are exhausted and tired the majority of the time. You may have a higher tendency of feeling sick, lots of headaches, muscle aches, and back pain. Some people that endure mental exhaustion for a long period will sometimes see some changes in their sleep habits and appetite.
- ❖ Emotional symptoms: If the emotional symptoms show up, you may have feelings of being helpless or like you are trapped and defeated by all of the mental stress you are under. The sense of self-doubt and failure can take over a lot of your thoughts at all parts of the day, which means that you are more likely to isolate yourself and then develop a more pessimistic view of the world, and of your life, in general.
- ❖ Behavioral symptoms: It is common for those with mental exhaustion to spend less time with their family and friends because they are just

too tired and worn out to make the effort. If you notice that you are procrastinating more often and you are withdrawing from some of your other responsibilities, this can be a sign as well. You may notice that some of your eating habits change, sometimes you'll eat more, and sometimes you'll eat less. Depending on the individual and the severity of the mental exhaustion, the use of drugs or alcohol to cope with the extra stress is a sign that you need to watch out for as well.

For the most part, mental exhaustion is not something that is going to occur in a big fell swoop and all at once. It usually is going to accumulate over time. Being overworked, having too much to handle during the day, or just having too many things going on in your life can cause you to reach a boiling point, or the point where the body and the mind just aren't able to cope anymore. When this happens, you will start to see the symptoms show up.

All of us think that we are invincible and can handle as much stress as we want. But at some point, the stress is going to be too much. When we reach our capacity for dealing with stress, it can push us into a state of mental fatigue. In some cases, this brings about many health issues including chronic illness, autoimmune disorders, heart disease, and depression.

The good news is that there are ways that you can recover from mental exhaustion. It is amazing how resilient the body and mind can be, and are able to repair themselves from the injuries and symptoms that come from mental exhaustion. The biggest challenge here is that you must admit that you need to make a change. This helps you to not feel so guilty about making the change and helps you recharge your energy. Some of the other things that you can do to help yourself and your mind recover from mental exhaustion include:

1. Find some time to relax: Often stress is going to accumulate and take over because we don't take time for ourselves and time to relax. If

there isn't an outlet to relieve stress in your life, it will just stay around and just compound, causing a bunch of stress related symptoms. Finding even a few minutes a day to collect your thoughts and relieve stress can help you out so much. Taking a bath, reading a book, going on a walk, or just sitting quietly on your own can all help with this.

2. Reduce any sensory stimulation: Being around a lot of extra light and noise can really bombard the senses, which will lead to more stress. Your body is going to feel its most relaxed when you sit down in a dimly lit and quiet room, with as few distractions as possible. All of the constant sensory stimulation that comes from our phones and our screens can cause eye fatigue, headaches, and insomnia. If you need a sensory reset, consider going camping or visiting a park for a bit to help out.

3. Learn how to prioritize: Not all things are going to be worth your time to do. Sometimes the things that are the most unimportant are going to be the biggest contributors to your levels of

stress. Recognizing the things that are actually important, and then letting go of the rest can help alleviate some of the mental exhaustion that you may be feeling.

Remembering Names and Faces

There are a lot of different ways that our mind can start to cause us problems and our memory can start to fail us. But many times people will have trouble with either faces, names, and numbers. Whether you deal with memory issues on all three of these, or just on one or two, it can be frustrating and can even cause problems in your personal and professional life. If you have some trouble remembering these things, you're not alone. There are many people who struggle with this issue, and often it is because the brain is wired to remember faces better than names. Often the best thing that you can do to help with this problem is to pay attention, and to use some different tricks to ensure the memory can do its job.

The first thing that you need to do is pay attention to the name. One of the best ways to learn the name of a person is to pay attention and really use your concentration when you hear the name for the first time. You can repeat the name a few times in your head to help it sit in your memory. Any time that you are in a situation where you meet someone, you may find that you get caught up in the moment, and you won't pay as much attention to their name as you probably should. During this time, you want to make sure that the name is actually able to enter your mind, rather than having it go in one ear and out the other.

If you find that you got caught up in the situation and you don't remember that person's name, even while in the same situation and conversation, then make sure to ask for it again. Most people won't mind telling it to you again, and this is another way to ensure that you can remember the name later on.

Another thing that you can do is after someone introduces themselves to you, stop and repeat their name right away. It doesn't have to be awkward, simply saying something like "Hello, Abby, nice to meet you" can help you to say the name again without making things sound strange. Being able to repeat the name out loud can solidify it in your brain because now you have said it and heard it. You may also want to say the name again, one or two times, to help you solidify this a bit more.

Making associations with the name can work to your advantage as well. Sometimes you will have a better time remembering the name if you try to make an alliterative association back to the name. For example, if you meet someone named Joe and he tells you he is from Jonesville, you could say something, in your own head, like "Joe joins us from Jonesville. The repetition of J can help you to have a better time remembering the name.

You can also consider doing a bit of rhyming in the mix as well. If you are able to come up with something that rhymes with the name, it helps it stick in your in your memory. With the name of Joe that we used before, you could go with a rhyme of "Joe knows how to tow", especially if he owns a towing company. If nothing seems to come to mind, then you can use a visual cue and make something up that will help you remember a bit better.

There are some people who run into issues with numbers as well. Numbers, especially ones that are a bit longer, are always a challenge. Turning them into words can sometimes make a difference when you want to remember them. You could come up with your own system, such as 1 = A, 2 = B and so on. From there, you would just make up your own acronym for the letters you have, and that can help you remember even the longest of numbers.

Often we have to take a few extra steps to ensure that we remember names, faces, and numbers. They aren't just going to stick because we want them to. We may have to go through and add some meaning to them to help them make more sense to us.

How Focus, Concentration, and Observation Affect the Memory Process

Studies have found that the amount that you focus or concentrate on something, the easier it is to store that event or information in your memory. If you are having trouble remembering things, perhaps the main issue here isn't that your memory is lacking, but rather, it could be due to the fact that you aren't paying enough attention to the things that are going on around us.

There are several reasons why our focus may be out and why we may not be able to pay attention to the things that we should. The first issue is that our brains are wired to drown out a lot of the extra noise. There is just so much that goes on around us. If we actually tried to pay attention to it all, we would go insane pretty quickly. The mind has learned how to turn a lot of this off so that we can work on focusing on just what is important, rather than on all the other little things that aren't that important.

The problem comes when we stop focusing on anything. In our modern world, we are often so busy running from one thing to another, that our focus and concentration is on too many little things, rather than on the important things. This confuses the brain, and it may have trouble figuring out what it should pay attention to at all. The brain isn't suffering from memory problems—it is dealing with a lack of focus problem instead.

The mind is trained to block out a lot of things like certain noises, and events that go on around us. If our mind failed to do this, it would cause our lives to be somewhat of a struggle due to us always trying to take in a million things at once.

A good exercise that you can try out is to go out for a walk. During this walk, try to pay attention and focus on the things that are around you. Do you hear the birds chirping? Can you tell if there is more than one type that is making noise at the moment? Can you pay attention to the smells? Do you notice the smell of the freshly cut grass, the flowers, the air, and the sun? Can you feel the hard pavement under your feet, or perhaps you took your shoes off and can feel the softness instead?

Focusing your mind in this way, even for just a few minutes a day, can do some wonders when it comes to improving the memory that you have. This method allows you to retrain your brain, helping it to develop and teach it what to focus on and ultimately improving your memory as well.

Memory Recall

The recall or the retrieval of memory is going to refer back to the re-accessing of events or information from the past. These events and the information has already been encoded and stored in the brain at some point in the past. This is a process that we often refer to as remembering. During the process of recall, the brain is going to replay back for us a neural activity pattern, one that was generated originally in response to one event or another. This helps to echo back the perception the brain had about the event. This process is so similar to thinking that there isn't really much of a distinction between thinking and remembering.

Of course, the replays that you see are not going to be identical to what you saw with the original. If this were true, we would have trouble telling the difference and fall into an issue with mixed awareness as we wouldn't know the difference between the memory and the genuine experience. One way that the differences show up is that memories won't be frozen in time. There are new information and some suggestions that can become incorporated into some of your older memories as time goes on. This is why remembering is sometimes known as an act of creative reimagination.

Due to the manner in which memories are stored and encoded, you will find that memory recall can be a reconstruction of elements that have been stored in different parts of the brain. Despite what we have thought for years, memories aren't going to be stored like books in a library. They aren't even stored as a collection of video clips and pictures. Instead, they are like a collage where the various elements are stored in separate parts of the brain, and then they are linked back together through associations and neural networks.

When we want to recall a memory, there is going to be a need for revisiting the nerve pathways of the brain, the ones that were formed there when the brain encoded the memory in the first place. How strong these pathways are can determine how easy it is for us to recall that memory.

The efficiency that humans are able to recall their memories is pretty amazing. Many times the things that we work to remember will occur from direct retrieval, where items of information will be linked right to a cue or a question, rather than through a sequential scan like a computer is often going to use. Then there are memories that are going to be brought out with the help of hierarchical inference, where a specific question is going to be linked back to some information when you know certain facts. Sometimes, the brain has the power to decide ahead of time whether it is worth its time to search for a fact or a memory. For example, if someone asked you what Aristotle's telephone number is, the brain therefore would know that is silly and wouldn't work on trying to find the memory.

When it comes to memory recall, there are going to be two main methods that you can use including recall and recognition. First is recognition that is going to be an association of an event, or an object, with one previously encountered or experienced. This is going to involve some comparisons within the brain. This is often a process that we are unconscious about and the brain even has some areas that are solely dedicated to face recognition so that we can recognize others we have met before, without having to go through and search for the information.

Many times, recognition is going to be seen as a superior skill compared to recall mostly because it is a bit more effective. It only relies on one process instead of two. This is because the process of recognition is going to be a familiarity decision while a full recall is going to require a search and retrieval of the item from the memory. From there, the recall process will rely on the familiarity decision to ensure that you pick the right answer to form the choices.

It is possible to increase the efficiency of memory recall in some cases, simply by making some inferences from our personal stockpile of knowledge about the world, and by the use of schema in the process. To help here, a schema is going to be an organized mental structure of pre-conceived ideas about the world around us and how this world works. We can then use this information to make assumptions that are realistic and that helps us to interpret the world that is around us.

With that said, there are going to be three different types of recall that are important to know about. These include:

1. Free recall: This is the process where a person is given a list of the items they need to remember, and then they will be asked to recall those items in any order they want. This is going to be the recall you use to display evidence of either the primary effect, which is when the person is able to recall items presented at the beginning of the

list earlier and more often, then it shows the recency effects as well, when the person is able to recall the items that were at the end of the list better. Sometimes the contiguity effect is going to occur though, which is a tendency of the individual for items from neighboring positions on the list to be recalled the most successfully.

2. Cued recall: This is a process where a person will be given a list of items that they need to remember. When they are tested, they will be given guides and cues to happen. When the cues are provided to these test subjects, they are more likely to remember the items on the list, even if they had trouble before. This can also be done with the stimulus response recall. This is when numbers, pictures, and words are shown on a page together to help you remember things better.

3. Serial recall: This is the ability of some people to recall events or items in the order that those things occurred. This would include events that were chronological or autobiographical

memories. It can even include things like the ordering of sentences to help them make sense. Serial recall that occurs in the long term memory is going to be different compared to those that show up in the short term memory. When serial recall has been tested, there are several general rules that are going to show up including:

    a. Events that are more recent are the ones that are easier for people to remember.

    b. The recall is going to decrease if the list or the sequence starts to increase.

    c. There is going to be a tendency to remember the correct items, but the order is often going to be harder to get right.

    d. When there are errors being made, there is sometimes a tendency of the individual to respond with an item that resembles the original item in some way. So, they may say dog instead of fog if they were given a list of words to remember.

e. Sometimes there are going to be errors in repetition, but these are often pretty rare.

f. If the person recalls an item on the list earlier than it was listed, then there is a tendency to insert the missed item right after.

g. If an item from a previous trial is recalled during the current trial, it is more likely to be recalled at the position it was at in the original trial.

Memory recall is a process that everyone goes through when they want to be able to remember or bring out a memory after the mind has already gone through and encoded that memory. Being able to do this recall can make it easier to bring out old memories and information at any time that we need. For those who have trouble with recalling items, there is often an issue with the encoding process, and that is the first thing they need to explore and try to fix.

Let's Test Your Memory

Now we are going to get started on a simple test that you are able to use in order to help test out your memory and how well it is doing. This is just a basic one to get you thinking about how well your memory is doing. You can go through and try out some other options later as you practice your memory and work to get better. There are many options online that you can use as well.

For the following questions, answer these with the following answers:

Always- 1

Often- 2

Sometimes- 3

Rarely- 4

Almost Never -5

Let's get started.

1. Do you find that it is often hard for you to remember phone numbers and the names of people you meet?
2. How often do you have to stop and try to remember where you placed everyday items? This can include options like your wallet, keys, glasses, and more.
3. How often do you have to go through and replace the passwords that you have, whether verbal or numerical, because you can't remember what the original one was?
4. How often do you stop and ask yourself "What was I about to do next"?
5. How often do you end up double-booking or scheduling yourself, because you forgot that you had previous plans in place with someone else?
6. How often do you need to ask someone near to you to repeat instructions or even a story that they were telling you simply because you weren't able to remember what they told you the first time?

7. How often do you have trouble when it comes to remembering where the car is parked?

For this test, the lower the score the worse your memory is at this time. This means that you almost always, or often, forget important and everyday things like where your keys are or the names of people you meet. The higher your score, the better your memory is. For this test you should have had a test score of somewhere in between 25-35. This would of shown you that your memory is ok and of average. Anything below might give you the indication that you need to try and focus on sharpening your memory skills up for the future

But before you start fretting and no matter what you scored in the test, there are things that you can do in order to improve your memory. All of us need help with our memory at some point, and this test just gives you a realistic idea of where you are starting so you can make the right changes.

We will take a look in the next chapter at some of the different techniques that you can use to help improve your memory. If you take a few tests, including the one above, and you are not happy with the results that you get, don't be upset with yourself. Using the different techniques that we discuss in this guidebook will help you to get your memory to a higher level, no matter where you were at the beginning of this journey.

Chapter 3

Memory Improvement Techniques And Exercises

Now that we have spent some time talking about human memory and how it works, it is time to look at some of the ways that you can improve your memory as well. Seeing improvement when it comes to our memory's ability to remember things, is something that we would all like. Remembering things such as names, faces, and facts, with ease is something that would make life so much easier. With the techniques that are presented next, you will be able to gradually improve your memory as time goes on.

Stop Multitasking

Multitasking is something that we are taught to do at a young age and is something that we are pretty used to working with. We often think that it is the best way to get as much done as possible in a short amount of time. With how busy we are in our daily lives, we figure that the only way to keep going and not fall behind, is to simply just multitask.

There are many studies out there that talk about how bad multitasking can be for you. It may seem like a great idea, and one of the things that you need to do to stay on top of things, but this is simply not true. Not only is it really slowing down the work that you need to complete compared to doing each task on its own, but it is also making it hard on your memory to remember what you need.

Multitasking is the shorthand for individuals to try and do as many things at the same time as possible. In the long run, the process of multitasking can actually slow you down, can make you very forgetful, and even makes you more prone to errors as you go along.

In fact, research has shown that you need at least eight seconds to memorize most things. So, if you are talking on the phone to someone, carrying in the groceries, and put your car keys down whilst doing these things, it isn't very likely that you will remember where you have put them.

It is much better for your memory to avoid doing multitasking as much as possible. Instead of working with multitasking, you should consider working with mindfulness. Mindfulness is going to help you to achieve a focus that is undistracted. For example, students who decided to take a class on mindfulness found that they were able to score better on reading comprehension as well as their capacity for working memory. These students also found that they had fewer thoughts that distracted them from the task at hand.

If you end up in a situation where you are trying to work on five tasks (or more at the same time, it is a good idea to stop yourself. Instead of focusing on all five, make sure that you focus your attention on the task at hand. If you notice that a thought that is distracting starts to enter your head, remember that these aren't really reality, and try to not think about them by just focusing on the thing you were doing. You may even want to consider ending the day with a short meditation session so that you can work on stopping the wandering of your mind which will also help you to relax, and ensures that you get a more restful sleep at night.

Focusing Your Attention

You will find that one of the major components to your memory and remembering various things is attention and what you focus that attention on. To ensure that the information you want to hold onto is able to move over from the short term to the long term memory, then you must attend to this information. There is just too much going on around you for the brain to focus on everything. Often this means that the mind will have to pick and choose what information it wants to hold onto, and which information you will ignore.

Sometimes this means that you need to override the mind and choose what needs your attention. You can decide what is important and then focus all of your attention onto it, alerting the mind that this is something you want to remember in the future. One of the best ways that you can focus your attention is to make sure that you learn the information without a lot of distractions. Some of these distractions are easy to avoid, such as turning off the music, turning off the television, and ensuring that your computer and your phone won't cause a distraction to you. Other times, avoiding distractions, such as noisy children or your roommate, can be quite hard. You may need to find some time to be alone to do memorization or find another place to be during that time.

Avoiding Cramming

This is something that you can use if you need to get ready for a big test at school, but it can also be helpful if you have a big presentation that you need to give at work. In fact, it works no matter what situation you end up in where you must remember a lot of information in order to prepare for that specific situation at hand.

Cramming is one of the worst things that you can do. Remember that the memory is only able to hold onto about seven items at one time. You can do chunking and organization and other options in order to help hold onto new information as well. Mnemonic devices are something that can help you hold onto more information also. But there is a limit to how much the brain is able to hold onto during a specific period of time. The brain has its limits and by cramming too much information into it, especially at one time, it will usually hit a limit and struggle to take in any more.

It is much better to study material over several sessions, with these sessions spaced out far enough apart. This allows you to keep filling up the brain, without overdoing the amount that it is able to handle. Research has shown over and over again that students who study on a regular basis, for shorter sessions are able to remember the material a lot better, often leading them to do better on tests than other who don't.

Be Organized and Structured

When you are surrounded by chaos, it is hard to concentrate on tasks, and things you are trying to do.

Disorganization and clutter are often things that will distract you, due to drawing you from what you were doing, to wanting to clean up the mess and tidy up. This will often lead to things that are really your priority to get done, getting postponed as a result of this.

Researchers have found that information organized inside of the memory in clusters are related. You are able to use this information to your advantage if you structure and organize all of the material that you are trying to study. For example, you may find that it is useful to group together concepts and terms that are similar. Or you may want to make a good outline of your readings and notes so that you can go back through and group together the concepts that are related.

Relate the Information Back to Things You Know

No matter what, there are already situations and people you know in your life. Whether they are something from your past or something that you are very familiar with now, you can use this to your advantage to help you improve your memory. This is really helpful if the material you are trying to learn is unfamiliar and you need some help with remembering it in your own life.

When you are working with material that is really unfamiliar to you, take some time to think about how that particular set of information can already relate to information that you know. When you are able to establish a good relationship between the ideas that are new and the previously existing memories, this will help you ensure that you are going to recall the information a lot easier.

Read the Information Out Loud

The more times that you are able to rehearse the information, the easier it is for you to remember. When you are trying to learn something new, especially if it is something that is difficult to remember, you may find that reading it out loud will help it sink in better. This may be due to the fact that not only are you reading the words on the page, but you are hearing them as well when your voice goes over them.

Research suggests that reading new information, or other reading materials, out loud, can significantly improve how well you are able to remember the material. Both psychologists and educators have found that when students have to learn new material, they are able to understand the information and recall it later better than before, after doing this. It has proven to leave a secondary blueprint of the information for the memory to store.

Trying Meditation

Meditation is a technique that can help you to calm down your mind and reduce stress that you may have built up. It may not directly work on the memory like some of the other techniques, but since it works on things like clearing the mind, introducing mindfulness, reducing stress, and leaving you overall feeling more relaxed, it can work wonders for helping you free up your mind, and make more room for you to remember things, in the future.

There are a ton of benefits that come with meditation. Just by reducing the amount of stress that you feel on a regular basis, and helping you learn how to slow down and relax, meditation can prevent many health conditions that may be plaguing you. There are a lot of different methods of meditation that you can choose to work with, which makes it easier to find one that you like and suits you.

You can do meditation on your own, or if you'd prefer you can always choose to go with guided meditation instead. Most of the time the meditation session should be in a quiet environment with no sound, but you may use some soft music or utilize a word or mantra to help you have something to focus on.

If you want to utilize meditation to help with your memory, there are a few different methods that you can try. We are going to take some time to look at one of the basic meditation sessions that you can do. It is very simple and it can last as long as you want it to, but going for at least five to ten minutes is usually ideal to help you relax and get the full benefits.

To start with, make sure that you are able to sit in a place that is quiet and where you can be left alone for at least ten to fifteen minutes. You will want to sit down on the floor and get comfortable. Have your legs crossed, your back stacked nice and straight so that the air from breathing can easily fill up your lungs. Leave your hands on your lap. If sitting on the floor is not comfortable for you, it is fine to either put a cushion underneath you to keep your alignment right, or you can sit in a chair if you want, as long as your back stays straight and your feet are on the floor.

When you are ready to start, take in some deep and cleansing breaths and then close your eyes. Try to keep your mind clear, and just focus on the deep breaths that you are taking in and out. As a beginner, this can be fairly hard at first. Your mind will try to drift on to the things that have been happening and going on in your life, such as work, family life, and events. But try your best to keep all the memories and thoughts out of the way and keep your mind as clear as possible.

If thoughts start to creep into your meditation, try not to get mad or down about yourself. This will just make it harder. When those thoughts get into your mind, you will just need to gently push them aside to help clear your brain from this kind of thinking. This can take some practice, but the more that you work on the meditation process, the easier it is for you to accomplish this goal.

When the ten to fifteen minutes are done, you can take a few more deep breaths, and then slowly open your eyes. You can then get up and move on with the rest of your day. It is best if you can do at least one meditation session each day. It is up to you how long you would like it to last, whether you would like to do it in the morning or evening, whatever works well for you.

Live a Life That Is Blessed and Happy

The happier and healthier you are able to live your life, the better your memory is going to become. The lesser negativity you have in your life the more this will boost your memory and help you to recall more. There are several different things that you can do to help make this happen, and working to implement each one will do wonders when it comes to your memory and how well it works.

The first thing that you will want to do is make sure that you can get your life organized. A life that is disorganized and cluttered can bring about a lot of forgetfulness. You should spend some time organizing your home and your office. Everything that is there either needs to have its own personal place, if you have things that are not essential and needed, it would be ideal to remove these things. You can choose to use a day planner or your smartphone to take notes on tasks, appointments, and other events that are going to happen during the week so you stay as organized as possible.

You may also find that taking notes and writing down any information that is important, such as meetings, names, and discussions that you don't want to forget can help reinforce the power of learning and remembering, even down the line. In addition to writing down the information, consider repeating the information or the name out loud, at least once when you first hear it like we have talked about previously.

Socializing can be an important aspect of this as well. People who isolate themselves and only go out on occasion will often miss out on the socialization aspect that is needed. Spending time with others, conversing with them, and learning new things for these individuals can go a long way in helping you to keep the mind sharp. A rich and full social life can help to prevent depression and stress and keeping your social calendar as full as you can will help prevent a decline in memory.

Another thing that you can try when you are working to live a life that is blessed and happy is to laugh more. Unlike other emotions that you may experience, laughter is able to engage more than one region of the brain and research has shown that it can also be beneficial to your memory. The more time that you spend laughing during the day, the better your memory will be.

There are many ways that you can work to improve your memory through laughter. You may want to try to join a Laughter club and participate as much as possible. You may want to spend time with children enjoying their stories and fun ideas. You can surround yourself with people who are playful, fun-loving, and like to laugh as well. Maybe try putting up some funny pictures around your home that will at least make you smile when you see them. Try watching something that is funny like a comedy program or movie, in the morning or before bed to ensure that you get at least a little bit of laughter into your day, to help brighten up your mood.

Getting Enough Sleep

Harvard Research shows that people are 33 percent more likely to infer connections among ideas that are related distantly after they sleep. But what is really interesting is that few realize that their performance got better after they slept. Sleep can also help to make your memories more effective and can help you practice and improve your performance when it comes to some of your more challenging skills. In fact, it only takes one night of getting no more than six hours of sleep in order to impact how clearly you are able to think the next day.

We have all had this happen at some point, when we have to stay up late due to things like studying, socializing with friends or trying to get our kids to sleep, causing us to get a lack of sleep. The after effect of this will usually cause us to forget things easily and lead us to make a lot of mistakes as we stumble through the day. Often that day is much harder to get through compared to some of the others, and we can't wait to just get it over with so we can go back to sleep.

The process that is known as neuroplasticity, or brain growth, is believed to underlie the capacity and the ability of the brain to control behavior. This includes our memory and how we learn. Plasticity is going to occur when the neurons start to receive stimulation from the information, for events, or from the environment that is around us.

In addition, there are certain types of long-term potentiation, that can be elicited in sleep. The potentiation is going to be a neural process that is going to be associated with the laying down of memory and learning. This suggests that the connections between the synapsis are going to become stronger when you get to sleep. Not sleeping enough, will cause these connections to not form as well as before.

This is also something that applies to infants. Research shows that even small naps can be what the baby needs in order to boost their brainpower. In specific, infants who slept in between their learning and then their testing sessions, found that they had a better ability to recognize patterns in new information. This showed researchers that there is a big change in memory that can help with the cognitive development of the baby.

It is believed that this can be the same for many adults too. It is believed that taking a nap in the afternoon could help to restore and boost your brainpower. Plus, it can make things easier if you are lacking in sleep at night because of other things going on. What this means is that if you are looking to boost your cognitive power, going to bed early, or taking a nap in the afternoon, may be the best way to make this happen.

Playing Brain Games

Playing brain games is another way to stretch your mind allowing it to work harder than it has done before. If you don't spend some time to challenge your brain the proper way with surprising and new information, over time it is going to start to deteriorate. What the research about brain plasticity shows us is that when we provide the brain with the right kind of stimulus, then you will have the key to counteract the degermation that would normally happen.

There are a variety of methods that you can use in order to add in a challenge for the brain including methods such as using brain games. You can find these on a variety of websites, they will usually give you scores at the end so you know how well you have done. A good website like Lumosity.com is a great place to start.

Dr. Michael Merzenich, a professor emeritus at the University of California, is one of the pioneers of research into neuroplasticity and brain plasticity for over 30 years. He has been able to develop brain training programs for the computer that can help you to work on a large range of memory and mental skills such as improving memorization and reading comprehension. This is a program that is known as Brain HQ which has a ton of exercises that you can use to help you work on your memory, to increase your mental power, and even allows you to keep track of the progress that you are making over time.

Some people will like to spend their time doing things like word finds or Sudoku and crossword puzzles, to help build up their memory. These are things that can be done from anywhere and at any time, and are things that can help you out a lot.

If you do decide to implement brain games into your routine to improve your memory, then it is ideal if you invest a minimum of 20 minutes a day on this. Of course, make sure that you divide that up between a few different tasks, such as five to seven minutes per task, as spending too much time on one task is not beneficial.

According to Dr. Merzenich, whom we have mentioned previously, the primary benefits are going to show up in the first five minutes or so of doing the task. Any longer than this and you will risk getting bored or mental fatigue, therefore not letting you reap the benefits.

Of course, you should only really be doing brain games if you find that they actually stimulate and interest you. For some people, these tasks are just going to be another thing that they need to be able to fit into their schedule. They may find them boring and no fun at all. If this sounds like you, don't try to force yourself into doing them. You need to focus on things that are interesting and stimulating for yourself. If the brain games don't do it for you, consider working on a new skill or hobby, or find another option to help you out.

Master a New Skill

One thing that you may want to try out when you are working on improving your memory is including mastering a new skill. Your mind is always looking for something new to learn, as it gets tired of learning the same thing over and over again. Over time, you will find that the memory just kind of stagnates, rather than grows, which can cause you to lose memory instead of improving it.

Engaging in a meaningful and purposeful activity, it is going to do wonders when it comes to stimulating your neurological system. Doing this can also help things such as, countering the effects of any diseases related to stress, reducing your risk of developing dementia, and enhancing your wellbeing and health. Just simply working on mastering a new skill, will allow you to challenge your mind in the way it needs.

A key factor in helping you improve the functioning of your brain, or even reversing some of the functional declines is the seriousness of purpose with which you engage in a new task. What this means is that you can't just go sit there mindlessly in a class on a new subject, without feeling any care or passion about that topic. The task needs to be something that is important and somehow interesting and meaningful to you. Something that will actually challenge you and get your attention.

One study found that doing various craft activities, such as knitting and quilting, were associated with a decreased likelihood of having mild cognitive impairment. This is good news for those who want to make sure that your mind stays sharp, even as you age.

There is another study that was published that found that spending at least a little of your time doing an activity that was cognitively demanding, such as digital photography, learning a new language, or even learning how to quilt, can help to enhance the functioning of the memory. Any activity can work as long as it keeps the mind active and will hold your interest for an extended period of time.

The key here is to find some kind of activity that is stimulating for your brain. This means that it must be an activity that will require your undivided attention while also giving you some satisfaction for doing the work. It also needs to be some kind of activity that you are excited about and are going to look forward to doing. You can choose the activity that you want to go with, as long as you pick one that is going to challenge your mind in some way that you are not used to. Some of the different activities that you can try out include things like crafting, building, gardening, language learning, or playing an instrument.

Trying Mnemonic Devices

Another option that you can work with is a mnemonic device. These are techniques that you are able to use to help you improve how well you remember something. It is basically a memory technique that you can use to help your brain encode and recall information. It is just a simple shortcut that can help you to associate the information that you need to remember with a word, sentence, or an image depending on what works the best for you.

Mnemonic devices have been around for a long time and some of them can be dated back to the time of ancient Greece. Almost everybody already uses them, usually without even realizing. It is a simple way for you to help memorize information so that you can recall it later on when you need it a lot easier.

There are actually quite a few different types of mnemonic devices that you can choose to use. Each of them can be effective, but it will depend on your overall goals and what you are hoping to get with memorizing the information. Some of the most popular mnemonic devices that you can choose to use to help your memory includes:

The Method of Loci

This is a mnemonic device that originated from back in ancient Greek times, and is one of the oldest methods of memorizing that we know how to use today. This method is an easy one to work with. To do this, imagine in your head a place that you are pretty familiar with already. You can use something as simple as your home. The rooms in your house will become the objects of information that you need to memorize. Or you can choose to use the route that you usually take to get to school and work. Then you can use things to memorize along the way such as the landmarks.

With this method, you are going to go through a list of concepts and words that you need to memorize and then try to associate every word with one of the locations. You need to make sure that you have this in some type of order, so that you can retrieve all of the information that you need in the future.

Acronyms

Another skill that you can work with when it comes to mnemonic devices is an acronym. This is going to be a word that is formed with the first letters, or groups of letters, that show up in a phrase or a name. You can also work with an acrostic, which is a series of lines from which a particular letters form into a phrase or a word. This could include the first letters that come from all of the lines. You can use these as a type of mnemonic device by taking the first letters of words, or you can pick names that you need to remember and then develop your own acrostic or acronym.

Let's look at an example of this. In music, many students are going to have to learn the order that the notes are there to make it easier to identify and play the right note when the music is read. The notes that show up on the treble staff are going to be EGBDF. And the acrostic that is often used with this is going to be Every Good Boy Does Fine. Then when we look at the bass staff, the notes are ACEG. This one is often going to be the acrostic of All Cows Eat Grass.

You can always choose to make your own acronym based on the information that you are trying to remember. Keep the words in the order that you need to remember them by. This helps you to make an acronym that makes sense for your needs and ensures that not only do you remember the words or the information that you need but that you remember it in the right order.

Rhymes

A rhyme is a saying that is going to have a similar terminal sound when it gets to the end of every line. They are the way that we used to learn things when we were younger, and they can still be used often as adults if we just learn how to work with them the right way. Rhymes are often seen as easier to remember because you not only get to remember the words, but they can be stored by acoustic encoding in your brain. Some examples of the rhymes that you may want to work with include:

In fourteen hundred and ninety-two, Columbus sailed the Ocean Blue.

Thirty days hath September

April, June, and November

All the rest have thirty-one

Save February, with twenty-eight days' clear

And twenty-nine each leap year.

If you have a lot of information that you have to remember for something, then a nice rhyme can always be helpful. You have to be pretty creative to make this happen, and you may need to look at some examples online or ask others to help you find the rhyming words that you need to make this work.

Organization and Chunking

The next option that you can work with is known as chunking. This is an easy way for you to break down some big pieces of information into smaller and more organized chunks so that you can manage the information easier than before. A good example of this technique is how telephone numbers in the United States are listed. There are ten digits for each number, and then they are broken down into three chunks. This makes it much easier to remember the phone number, rather than hoping that you can remember ten random numbers.

For most people, the short term memory is going to have some limitations, and this is usually about seven items of information. Because of this, being able to place the larger quantities of information into the smaller chunks or the smaller containers, will make it easier for the brain to hold onto.

You will find that organizing the information that you have into either subjective or objective categories can help out quite a bit. When you use objective organization, you are basically placing the information into well-recognized and logical categories. For example, grass and trees would go into plants, and crickets would be an insect.

You can also choose to work with what is known as a subjective organization. This is when you make categories of items that don't seem related, but you do it in a way that makes it easier to recall the information later. This is a useful skill to work with because it will take the information that you need to learn and then enable you to break it down. If you are able to divide a list of items into a few categories, then all you need to remember is the categories in order to remember the rest of the information.

Imagery

The last type of mnemonic device that we are going to explore is that of imagery. Visual imagery is going to be a great way for a lot of people to memorize different types of items. For example, you may use it in order to help you to memorize a pair of words, such as green grass, yellow sun, and blue water. If you are using the Method of Loci that we talked about before, it is possible that you are using some kind of imagery to help with memorization. When you are able to recall specific imagery, it is going to help you out quite a bit if you are able to recall information that is associated with some kind of imagery.

This method can work best when you want to remember smaller pieces of information. When you are trying to remember the name of someone you just met for example, you may want to try and use imagery. You might meet someone with the name of Peggy and then imagine a pirate with a wooden leg. Or maybe if you met someone named Harry, you may imagine a big grizzly bear. You can choose the imagery that you want to use for each item that you need to remember. But since the brain and the mind work well with images and pictures, it is one of the best methods to help you get the most out of your memory.

As you can see, there are many different options that you can choose to use in order to improve the brain and ensure that you are able to remember anything that you want, whether it is big or small. By trying out a few of these different techniques to determine which ones work and don't work for you.

The 4 Details Exercise

This is a good one to work with when you meet someone new, and you want to make sure that you are able to remember them. For this, when you encounter someone new, try to memorize a minimum of four details about that person. It doesn't have to be anything too complex. Maybe you remember that they wore black shoes, a big hat, had red hair and wore a pink coat. The goal here is to observe some details about that person, so that you can recall those details easier later in order to help you remember.

There are some scientists who see this as more of a passive memory technique. The reason being is that you are not relying on just a special technique. Instead, your just asking the brain to do the work for you. The reason that this is so important is that we often don't ask the mind to practice being observant enough. Because of this, we often fail to observe what is going on around us. We may also fail to observe the things that we don't see, such as making a visual image of any movement that we may be able to hear in other rooms that are near us.

If you are looking to be a better observer of the things that are occurring around you, then this is the best exercise that would help you. This is also something that you can scale. Maybe you will start with an observation of just one new person for the day. After time and when you become more experienced, you can then add in more information, more people, or a combination of both depending on what you are the most comfortable with.

Number Brain Exercises

One thing that a lot of people struggle with when they are working on their memories is remembering numbers that they need. Numeracy is a skill that is really important, and it is something that you definitely need to work on each day when your trying to strengthen your memory. One technique that you can use is the add 3, minus 7 exercise technique. It's pretty simple to use, and will get the brain working when it comes to numbers, so it is definitely something that is worth trying out.

To get yourself started with this technique, just pick out any three-digit number. Then you will add three to the digit, doing that three times. Then you will take that new number and minus seven from it, seven times.

This means remembering all of the numbers you have chosen.

Keeping the numbers in order can be quite a challenge for your brain, but this will help in improving it, and when it comes to remembering things in the future.

You should try to do this exercise at least five times when you're trying it out for the first time. You can also add more digits, such as moving up to a four-digit number instead. If you want, you can also change up the numbers that you want to use, such as adding 12, 12 times and then minus 11, 11 times based on how much you want to progress and modify this exercise.

Doing Recall in Your Mind

While it is often best to say things out loud to help you remember them, there are some situations where this isn't ideal. Instead try to do the recall in your mind so that you can still say it, without looking silly in front of others.

You can simply follow any of the words that the other person is speaking by repeating those words in your own mind.

Now, imagine that you are in a conversation with someone, and they are telling you how they want to go to the movies tomorrow and see a new movie that has just come out. All you would need to do is repeat all of the words that the person uses to tell you about the movie, but repeat them in your head. This exercise works because you are asking your memory to recall information as it is happening. Of course, the more challenging the information that you ask the brain to keep up with, the more that you end up exercising the brain at the same time.

The Metronome Clapping Exercise

This is another great option that you can choose to work with. Try working with a Metronome if you happen to have one, or something similar, that can be just as ideal. But there are also videos online or other tools that you can use that work just as well. You can then set the metronome, or a similar sound, at a certain speed to then practice a technique that is known as covering the click.

While this one may not be as effective as some of the others when it comes to memory, it is going to work for improving your focus and your concentration. Both presence and concentration are going to be skills that we need to improve in order to help with the memory.

If you want to get better with this exercise, you may want to gradually increase the speed that the clicks happen. If you are able to start accurately covering the metronome with a long distance between the clicks, try speeding up the metronome in order to keep benefiting from this exercise.

Create Your Own Memory Palace

This is considered one of the best brain exercises that you can use, and is considered one of the easiest as well. All that it involves is making a simple drawing (you will make your own that no one is going to see, so don't worry about this). Of course, this simple drawing is going to have some principles that you need to follow in order to make this exercise work well.

So, why is a memory palace a powerful and effective exercise? First, the memory palace is going to work with some of your spatial memory. It can also be a good way to work on your autobiographical and recovered memory. When it comes to brain exercises, you will find that the memory palace is going to work in reverse to some of the other options that you work with. The reason for this is because you will access the cues that are already blueprinted on the mind, but may still be outside of your awareness.

While you may not be able to go into a brand new place or home and remember a ton of details, as if you were asked to remember the details of your own home or that of a friends. Creating a memory palace allows you to exercise the inborn ability that all humans have to remember certain details. Some people even use this idea to help when they are trying to remember or memorize something, such as trying to memorize all of the Prime Ministers of Canada.

Learn a New Language

This one is similar to learning a new skill or finding a hobby to keep you challenged, but you will find that learning a new language will be a great way to keep the mind sharp and working to its full potential. Bilingualism is perfect for the brain, and has been shown to improve cognitive skills, and also make you smarter.

Has there ever been a language that you might have been a little curious to learn? But never really had the time to do so? The good news about learning a foreign language is not only is it fun, but it can also help with your memory improvement. The main reason for this is that when you are learning a new language, you are continually asking the brain to bring out and recall information that you have previously learned.

You will find that learning a language is a great exercise for the brain not only because it provides a good challenge, but it gets you out there and talking and socializing with people. Regular conversation, especially in a new language, can be something that really stimulates the brain. You can increase the benefits of this further by even learning to sing in the new language. Singing has been shown to help increase cortisol and other chemicals that are needed for healing throughout the body. Because of this, learning a foreign language and singing it, at least sometimes, can help you increase the impact as well as the effectiveness of this kind of brain activity.

Working with a Mind Map

Mind mapping is usually a process that is done to help you make decisions and determine the best solution to get the results that you want. But you can utilize it in other aspects of your life to ensure that you keep the brain working as it should. Basically, you will start out with the problem that you want to fix, and then outline some of the various solutions that you think may work for it. You will keep going, following each course of action until you reach the one that makes the most sense.

The reason that the mind map works is that it forces you to stop and think about something critically. You aren't going to be limited by your emotions, and there will be a logical outcome that is based on facts and nothing else. You have to use this as a way to think in a more critical manner, learn how to come to a conclusion without any biases or emotions getting in the way. It is definitely a great way to think through some of the important decisions you often need to make.

Playing a Sport

As silly as it may seem, you will often find that playing a sport, especially a team sport where socialization is involved, can be a good way to improve your memory. But any type of sports activity in general such as things like working out at the gym with a partner can be highly beneficial also.

If you are doing something like just going to the gym and working out, you can make the brain work by memorizing the number of reps and sets that you need to do each time you train. You can also work on rehearsing the content of a program when you are on the treadmill. Or you can do the four detail exercise that we talked about before while observing some of the other people you encounter at the gym.

Working out at the gym can be a win-win. You get a chance to work out the body, meet new people, as well as using techniques to help improve your brain and memory at the same time.

As you can see, there are a ton of different techniques and brain exercises that you can choose to work with. Whether you are trying to use them in order to solve some of the real world problems that you are facing, or you are just trying to work with them in order to improve your memory, all of them can be used successfully. But this brings up the issues of which brain technique or exercise is the best one for you to use.

It is often going to depend on what issue of the memory you are trying to work on. Most of us have just one or two aspects that we will need to look into in order to improve. It is unlikely that we need to work on all aspects of the memory. Figuring out which areas of your thinking and your memory need the most improvement can help you to pick out the right exercises to do.

Since you are only supposed to spend about five minutes on each task, and for around 20 to 25 minutes a day on exercises, it is best to have at least a handful of techniques and exercises to help you out. You can set up a routine that you can follow on a daily basis, and then try to mix and match the exercises that will solve your particular memory problem, or the ones that work the best for your needs. There isn't really one particular memory exercise or technique that will work the best in every situation. You have to go through them all and pick the option that works the best for your needs and your own personal memory goals and then get started from there.

Chapter 4

Memory Improving in Your Day to Day Life

There are a lot of different things that you need to be able to remember during your day. These often include things like having to get the kids to school on time, remembering where you've put your keys, and important dates and appointments. But these can be basic things as compared to when you get to work and you have remember more complex things.

In addition to some of the techniques that we talked about above, there are a few daily routines that you can implement to help you improve your memory even more. These things can be as simple as starting an exercise routine, eating the right foods, playing memory games to keep the brain sharp, and socializing with those around you. Let's take a look at some of the basic things that you can do in your daily life to help you improve your memory in no time at all.

Exercising

The first thing that you can work on in order to improve your memory is exercising more regular. Exercising is one of the best things you can do for your whole body and your mind. Whatever type it maybe, exercise in general can be so beneficial when it comes to helping you in providing more oxygen and nutrients to your brain.

Many times as we age, we start to give up on exercising in our life. More than often we feel too tired and too weary to get up and get going. Other times we just may simply not have the time to do it. But other problems that may plague us like health issues, like pains and discomfort, weak bones, or balance problems. But there is always something out there you can do to suit you and your schedule.

Doing a wide range of exercises can be one of the best and beneficial ways to ensure that you are taking care of your mind as they all will play big factors towards improving it. Things like cardio and weight lifting has been shown to be good for the brain due to increasing the heart rate and getting more blood flow pumped to the brain.

Socializing

One thing to consider when you are working on your memory is that socializing can help. Being around others and talking with them can do wonders to ensuring your mind stays sharp and keeps working long into the future. A lot of the time we will be so busy with our own lives, we end up going long periods of time without talking to anyone else. This is a dangerous thing to get our-selves into because it can quickly lead to the decline of your mind.

This is another reason that some people may believe that their memories start to fade as they get older. As we age, we often find that our health and other factors force us to stay inside and maybe socialize less than we did in the past. But this is a bit of a dangerous thing to do. Socializing can help our brains stay sharp, but when we start to withdraw from society and from doing things that we enjoy, it is our mind and our memories that start to falter as a result.

Just doing the most basic of social activities will help you out a lot, such as going out for coffee with a close friend, joining a gym or doing some sort of evening classes. There is always something out there that will suit you, but always be willing try something new to help take your mind into new avenues, rather than keeping it to what it's already used to.

Keep Doing Mental Activities

A mind that is used on a regular basis is a strong mind, one that is able and willing to do anything that you ask of it. But a mind that sits there and just spends time on the computer or time watching television, is one that is going to waste away and will struggle with memory problems for many years to come. Regardless of your current mental activity level though, you can always add more of these activities into your routine to ensure that you make the mind as strong as possible.

Mental exercises can help to keep your brain working, and they don't have to be all that difficult. We have discussed previously of the many different exercises and things you can do such as puzzles, brain games and learning a new language.

While many people associate aging with the decline in their mental capacities, often the real issue lies more with their lack of working and exercising the brain. They will decide to sit at home and never try anything new or challenging. The mind needs to have a workout on occasion. It needs a chance to explore and learn new things. The more that you are able to do this, the less your memory is prone to fading over time.

Organizing Your Life

Sometimes the reason that we are not able to remember things is that our lives can be unorganized. The clutter around us can cause us to lose things, no matter how good our memory is. Taking some time to clear out the clutter and add some organization into your life could be the answer that you are looking for.

Clutter can cause us to become stuck thinking about mess, which can play a big role in our mental health. The messier a home is, the harder it is for our memories to work.

The best way to fix this problem is to learn how to cut down on the clutter as much as possible and implement some sort of organization into your life. The first step here is to go through the whole house, room by room if you have to, and start throwing things out. Many of us have a ton of stuff that just gets in the way and doesn't serve a purpose, or has lost its purpose that it once had.

This process can take some time, but once you declutter and get rid of many of the things that are just hanging around your home, taking up space and making it difficult for you to get things done in your daily life, you will be amazed at how much organization is implemented in. You can choose to either donate, sell, or throw away the items, just make sure that you get rid of as much as possible so the organization can begin.

Once your home is starting to look a little better, make sure that you give every item that you still have its own place. This not only makes the area look nicer and cleaner, as well as more organized, but it can do wonders for helping you to remember where things go so it's easier to find them later on. Try not to relapse when it comes to this, by cluttering up the newly cleared space with other things in the future.

Eating Well

The next thing that you can work on is making sure that you follow a diet that is healthy and full of nutrients that are good for you. The typical American diet is not good for the brain, as it doesn't feed the brain what it needs to work at its maximum capacity. The diet has even been proven to cause people higher levels of mental distress.

If you are currently on a diet that is high in sugars, carbs, bad fats, processed foods, and lots and lots of calories, like the typical American diet, then it is time to make some changes.

First, make sure that you take in plenty of healthy fruits and vegetables to start things off. There are many options that you can go with, and the more variety that you are able to add to your diet, the better. Fresh produce—and even the frozen variety—is full of great vitamins and minerals that can help your whole body function properly, and not just the brain.

You should always make sure that you take in lots of healthy carbs. There are some diet plans out right now that focus on how bad carbs can be for you, and how you should avoid them. This is somewhat true, as there are bad carbs out there, such as those found in baked goods and processed foods. But this doesn't mean that all carbs are bad. They can provide you with the sustainable energy that you need to keep going through the day.

Protein is also an important thing you need to consider. Try to take in healthy and lean sources of protein, like hamburger, chicken, turkey, and fish to get the protein and the healthy omega-3 fatty acids that the brain needs to keep your brain healthy. Try to get a few servings of this into your day and into each meal as well.

Dairy products are also an option. These products can make great snacks and provide you with calcium as well as protein. Maybe not the best option for those who are lactose intolerant, though there still is other alternatives such as things like coconut & soy milk etc.

Sleeping Well

It is important that you take the time to get plenty of sleep when you are trying to improve your memory. You will never see results if you only spend four to five hours a night, or even less, sleeping each and every night. This is in addition to feeling worn out, tired, and having lots of cravings for unhealthy foods. So much of our wellbeing is tied to getting enough sleep each night, but most of us are sorely lacking in it.

Sleeping will allow the mind to rejuvenate and rebuild. It lets the mind take all of the images, and events that has happened during that day, and selects those that are important for long term storage. Anything else will just get disregarded.

When the mind is not given enough sleep to let this process occur, then this is something that can affect your ability to remember things. Not only are you tired and worn out, but the brain hasn't been given enough time to store the memories or get rid of any.

If you are dealing with problems with your memories, then it may be time to consider changing up the sleep patterns that you have—and usually, this means that you need to start getting more sleep into your evenings. It is best to get about eight to nine hours of sleep each day so your brain is fully optimal. There are several things that you can do to make sure that you are getting the right amount of sleep each evening including:

1. Setting a bedtime to stick to. You will find that setting your own bedtime, and then sticking with it each and every night, can help you to get enough sleep. Figure out what time you need to be up in the morning, and then pick out a bedtime that is at least eight hours before

that. Stick with it all the time to ensure that you are getting the amount of sleep that your brain needs.

2. Work on a bedtime routine: A bedtime routine can help you to get the best results when it comes to falling asleep easier. This routine is going to signal to the brain that you are getting ready for bed so that it starts to wind down and is ready by the time you get yourself into bed. The bedtime routine doesn't have to take much time. Doing something simple like turning off the TV, brushing your teeth, getting into your pajamas, and reading for fifteen minutes can be exactly what you need to help shut the mind down for the night.

3. Turning off the lights: It is best for you to sleep in the dark. This is beneficial to the brain because it ensures that you are able to get to sleep. The brain is going to react based on whether it is light or dark. If you leave a lot of light near your room at night, the brain may think that it is daytime, and you won't be able

to sleep as well. Keep the room as dark as possible to facilitate the best sleep possible.

4. Limit screen time: The more that you can limit screen time before you head to bed, the better off you will be. The blue light that comes off your computer screen can make it really hard to fall asleep and studies have shown that it can definitely mess with REM sleep. It is best to turn off the computer and the television at least an hour before bed to give your brain a break and do something that can help you relax a little bit before you try to go to sleep. Also try wearing anti blue light emitting glasses if you spend a lot of time in front of the screen.

5. Try reading: Taking ten or fifteen minutes to read a little bit before you go to bed. This gives you a chance to calm the mind down and can be relaxing as well. Don't get into something that is too deep because this may have the reverse effect on you and make you stay up for longer. But finding something light and easy to read can be the thing you need to turn off the brain and makes it easier for you to fall asleep.

6. Play relaxing music. If you have trouble getting to sleep at night, make sure that you keep the television off. There are a lot of people who think that they need to keep the television on, but this is one of the worst things to do as it can really mess with your sleep cycle. If you find that you need some noise to get to sleep, consider getting some soft music to help. You can use classical music or even some quiet nature sounds to help you drift off.

Medications That Can Help with Memory Improvement

There are many people who are worried about their memory and how strong their brains actually are. People will try to make sure that they are doing everything possible to keep their brains sharp and to ensure that they don't have to worry about a host of neurological issues like dementia and Alzheimer's. If you feel that you need to do that bit extra to help support your brain, then you may be interested in looking to see if there are any supplements or other options to help with this.

But the biggest problem today with prescription drugs is that they normally come with a price tag, and they are often not as effective as they seem during a short window of time. This makes it hard for a lot of people to justify having them in the first place, causing them to just forgo them, or look for other options.

If you are looking for a supplement that will be able to help improve your memory, then you do need to be careful. There are some options that can be really helpful when it comes improving your memory, but many of them lack the right chemicals or research behind them to back up their claims.

When taking a supplement for your brain, you want to make sure that you are going with something that will actually work.

For example, there are a number of memory supplements on the market today that can potentially help the brain and memory. Some of the supplements that you should consider include:

- ❖ Omega-3 fatty acids: These are the lovely fats that come in fish oil supplements, and they have gained a lot of interest in recent years. You can find these in foods like cold water fish, oils, and some types of walnuts. This fatty acid has been linked to a lower risk of Alzheimer's in many individuals. There still needs to be more studies done to compare the Omega-3's to a placebo to ensure that this is something that is actually beneficial for this disorder.
- ❖ Huperzine A: This is sometimes known as Chinese club moss. It is a natural medicine that can often work in the body similar to how various Alzheimer's drugs do. There are a few questions about how safe and effective it is though.
- ❖ Acetyle-L-carnitine: There are some studies that will show how this type of amino acid can be beneficial in helping Alzheimer's patients with various memory problems. It can

sometimes provide a great benefit to people with early onset and a fast rate of the disease.

❖ Vitamin E: This vitamin can be useful in helping slow the progression of Alzheimer's. There has been recent studies that raised concerns about an increased risk of deaths in those who are unhealthy who start to take high doses of this vitamin. If you are worried about this, make sure that you talk to your doctor before you take this kind of supplement.

❖ Asian ginseng: This is a herb that can be used together with ginkgo biloba, which can help with your quality of life and fatigue. But there does need to be more studies done to prove whether or not this supplement is effective or not.

Chapter 5

Rebooting and Refreshing Your Brain

While the exercises that we talked about in this guide are going to do wonders for helping you increase the memory that you have, there are going to be times when you need to go through and reboot and refresh the brain—and one of the ways that you can do this is to work on the focus that your brain has. No matter how hard we try, there are going to be times when our focus isn't at its best.

There are many things that you can do to help you reboot and refresh the focus that your brain has on a daily basis. This chapter is going to look at some of the simple tasks that you can do, and most of them will only take a few minutes in order to make this goal a reality.

Mindfulness

Mindfulness and meditation are some of the best things that you can do no matter what your overall goals are. Whether you want to make sure that you see a reduction in the amount of stress that you feel, or if you would like to work on clearing the mind, slowing things down, or working on your memory, you will find that mindfulness is one of the best tools to work with.

Buddhists have been practicing mindfulness for centuries in order to experience the present that they live in with more balance. Working with mindfulness can help you to do that, while also increasing your focus and your concentration. When you spend time doing exercises related to mindfulness, you will learn how to direct all your focus and attention to a particular activity. Usually, this is a very simple activity, such as eating or smiling.

Let's say that you choose to focus your attention for a few minutes on smiling. To do this, you can sit with your eyes closed, and then do a slow smile. Make sure that you pay close attention to the different muscles of the face and how it moves when you smile. You feel the sensations on the lips, how the muscles tighten or relax. Your goal here is to bring attention over to the smiling if the mind does tend to wander off. You can end the focusing session after five minutes, but take a moment when you are done to reflect a bit on how that exercise felt.

Visual Tasks

Visual tasks are so important to the brain, and any time that you are able to tie information that you should remember to a visual, it is much easier for you to remember it. Attending to some kind of visual task can cause some firings in the visual cortex region of your brain. What this means is that these firings can help you keep out some of the distractions that you are facing and helps with focus.

According to Dr. Daniel T. Moore, you may be able to improve your concentration as well as your focus with a visual exercise that utilizes colored pencils. You will need to set your own timer, one that goes off at multiple random time intervals over five minutes. So, this may mean that the alarm is going to sounds after five seconds, and then again after 15, 10, and five.

When the timer is set, you can hold one pencil in each hand, making sure they are about 16 inches from the face and keep them shoulder-width apart. You need to focus exclusively on one of the pencils. Then, when the alarm does sound, you will want to focus the attention on the other. Switch where your focus is between the two pencils each time that you hear the alarm sound.

This is just one example of what you can do when it comes to working with a visual task. You may also find that working with other visuals can help as well. We discussed a number of these previously, but using your home as a way to store information, or adding a picture to the person when you remember their name can help you to remember them better than before.

Chewing Gum

Another thing that you may want to try out is to chew gum. The reason that this works is that the process of chewing gum can help you to use the attentional regions of the brain. This is a simple exercise where you will chew gum when you are doing a task that is work oriented or requires the brain to think when you are learning. This may include doing tasks like homework or attending a lecture with a lot of important information to remember.

Chewing gum has been shown to help students and others improve their ability to learn, and help them to retain and then retrieve the information that they need. An example that studies have shown that students who chewed gum while doing various math activities for a total of 14 weeks were able to achieve tests scores that were higher to those who didn't chew gum at all.

According to this study, which was done by the Baylor College of Medicine, the students who chewed gum were able to score about 24 and 36 percent higher than those who didn't chew gum on immediate word recall tests and delayed word recall tests respectively.

It has been proven in many studies that chewing gum actually helps with visual memory tasks and long- term concentration.

Belly Breathing

Sometimes the issue that you are dealing with is the fact that you are not breathing in the most efficient manner. Inefficient patterns in breathing can sometimes suppress how well you are able to focus and concentrate. This is because you may be limiting the amount of oxygen that enter your brain. If this is a problem you may think you have, then working on exercises that are known as belly breathing can sometimes help to improve your concentration and focus simply by correcting your patterns of breathing.

Belly breathing can help with things like boosting your IQ, providing more oxygen to the brain, and improving your learning efficiency.

To do this process, you just need to place one hand on your stomach and then inhale slowly through your nose, and into your stomach. You want to let the stomach expand for three seconds or so. After that time has passed, you can exhale for an additional three seconds, using your stomach muscles to push out the breath, rather than your diaphragm or your lungs. Spend at least a few minutes doing this, making sure that your stomach muscles do the work with the exhalation, to get the best results.

If you work on increasing your memory and using the various techniques that are out there to do this, then you will find that your focus is automatically going to increase as well. However, there are still going to be times when the focus and concentration you need will still be lacking. Working with some of the tasks and exercises above can help you get your focus back on track so that you can see the best results.

Conclusion

Thank you for making it through to the end of Memory Improvement! Let's hope it was informative and able to provide you with all of the tools you need to achieve your goals—whatever they may be.

Burt remember, our memories aren't fading because we are aging or because of things that we can't control. Oftentimes, the issue is because we just aren't challenging the brain and putting it to work. When this happens, the mind is going to start deteriorating, causing us to have the trouble remembering some of the very basic things that go on in our day. However, as we start to stimulate the brain more and get it to learn new things, or try something we have never tried before, then our memories will start to improve at the same time.

Dealing with a failing memory can be a difficult task. But in this book we have covered the basics of what you need to know about the memory, why it is important, and effective techniques and methods that you can apply to start improving your memory gradually.

Increasing our memories ability is something we all want to improve, and something we all can do. So make sure to take all the essential lessons and information you have learnt and apply it to your daily life.

Finally, if you found this book useful in any way, a review on Amazon is always appreciated!

www.ingramcontent.com/pod-product-compliance
Lightning Source LLC
Chambersburg PA
CBHW031118080526
44587CB00011B/1020